THOMAS GARDNER

SUNDAYS

Library of Congress Catalog-in-Publication data available upon request.
ISBN-13: 978-1-946482-35-8

Cover and text design by Erica Mena.
Cover art: *Spirit* by Margo Klass.

First paperback edition September 2020

Tupelo Press
P.O. Box 1767
North Adams, Massachusetts 01247
(413) 664-9611 / Fax: (413) 664-9711
editor@tupelopress.org / www.tupelopress.org

Tupelo Press is an award-winning independent literary press that publishes fine fiction, non-fiction, and poetry in books that are a joy to hold as well as read. Tupelo Press is a registered 501(c)(3) non-profit organization, and we rely on public support to carry out our mission of publishing extraordinary work that may be outside the realm of the large commercial publishers. Financial donations are welcome and are tax deductible.

FOR LAURA

SUNDAYS

2016-2017

1 | AUGUST 28

Walking with Laura at the pond. A few feathers and heaped up leaves all that remain of the nest we'd seen a Canada Goose building last Easter. It's down an embankment, just off the water, but you'd have to know where to look. We had watched her scooping leaves and twigs around her, then plucking feathers from her breast to line the nest, the male patrolling a few feet off shore. Three weeks after that, I'd watched my mother in the ICU in Burlington making essentially the same gesture—touching her blanket, pulling a loose corner toward her, bending and molding a green plastic bag and a straw wrapper into a rough nest, my father's eyes on the flashing numbers over her head. Her speech was like that too—the morphine, I think—eyes closed, a young girl sharing secrets, gathering up bits of the invisible, patting them into place. The mind moves this way, Wallace Stevens says, alone on a stage, speaking, insatiably, to its inner ear. Whispering to itself *peace* or *home*, plucking at its own breast and weaving what it finds there into something that might hold for a season or two. And what about us, Stevens's "invisible audience"? We lean forward in our seats, caught up in the work, listening. Rain falls over our heads. The dark night. The gliding figure in the water beside us.

Early morning walk, Deep Creek Lake in Western Maryland, alone. How odd to be back here, forty-five years after graduating from high school and leaving the area. Odder still, my best friend from high school called me this week, after finally tracking me down. He'd been searching for me for years, he said, but had been looking for the wrong person, or an earlier one. A chemical engineer, he thought. Or maybe a pastor. And here I was, teaching in Virginia only a few hours from where he lived. Would it be OK if he let a few people know he'd found me? Deep Creek is only about thirty miles from where I grew up and the mountains are very much the same. I've struggled to find myself too, I think, sitting now at the base of Wisp, staring up at the stilled lifts, Sunday a space to slow down and try to make something out of what comes near. Nothing. On the way back to where we are staying, a bit of swamp, now in the sun, catches my eye. I hadn't seen it before—gleaming jewelweed, cattails in the horizon, darting redwing blackbirds. "Often I am permitted to return to a meadow," Robert Duncan writes, in the first book of poems I ever carried around. Return how, I would wonder, getting lost for days in the idea that somewhere, "near to the heart," there was an "eternal pasture folded in all thought," and if you were someone like Duncan you could find your way back. After getting the news, one of our classmates emailed my friend a photo and he passed it on. 1970, the summer after we graduated. Five of us in a kind of circle, my head raised in Susie's lap, arm in a lazy peace sign. Laughter. Night sounds. The nearer faces are washed by the flash, the circle they form opening out to the viewer, as if to invite you in.

3 | SEPTEMBER 11

Sunday afternoon, the same blue sky of fifteen years ago, the trails deep in dust. Both ponds low and covered in small lily pads. Wildflowers tall and leggy, suddenly dying back. Shimmering yellow light. Duncan's line, borrowed from Pindar, shifts across my mind as it once did his, but there's nothing there to hold it: "The light foot hears you and the brightness begins." Duncan was reading late at night, and the line slipped free of its original context and called him out into a grand, free-wheeling dance, the *light foot* becoming a "god-step at the margins of thought," the *brightness* Psyche's lamp as she stood spellbound over the sleeping god who had come to her there. None of that today, though, just this shimmering insect wail. We circle the pond and, just before leaving it, slip down a track cut into the slope when they drained the pond and hauled off loads of sediment. The wail subsides. It's cooler down here. The surface of the water rises up like a wall of light. There's no horizon—the lily pads embedded in the light stare back like faces. Bare stalks where the flowers had been hiss and glow and drop a few embers of color like torches. I'm thinking of the Orangerie in Paris, that flat surface of light unfolding before us as if there were nothing else in the world, and holding ourselves there, a few steps back, at the just-articulated edge where paint gives way to light.

May Apple trail. I had run this yesterday, in the early dark. I remember the feeling of almost outrunning my headlamp—or not that exactly, the light bobbing a few steps ahead of where my feet were actually landing. The uneasiness of having to trust my body to take in what my brain couldn't fully register. Off the trail, an area beavers had flooded three or four years ago holds its green against the drying undergrowth surrounding it, pointed stumps ringing what had been a pond or swamp. A broken log crosses a nearly-dry stream bed, emptied into by ragged, leaf-filled gashes where spring torrents had run. The two of us chatting, the drying woods as we pass through them seemingly just out of reach, unfolding themselves to themselves. One of my students, I say, typed out sentences from Marilynne Robinson's *Housekeeping* on little squares of paper and pasted them on doors and windows and in the staircases of my building. Beautiful sentences, late at night. Imagine what it must have been like, moving from room to room, cutting spaces out of the emptiness and filling them with tiny squares of print, unfixed from narrative. The next morning, the entire building seemed ringed and veined with thought, all of us, together, turning in on ourselves and pressing down on some secret.

Walking the upper pond this afternoon and realizing how dry it's been. Almost no water at all, just rustling cattails and the drying out bottom, one shallow moving stream. Got very close to the beaver house near the center. It seems abandoned—no tracks in the mud, no signs of movement in or out. Yellow grass growing off the top, catching the sun. When my friend Tim fell off his bike this winter, slamming his head and breaking both wrists, it was as if he'd left something of himself out there, with no obvious way back. The first month was a single gray day, he said, with no working out where he was in it. When he was able to walk, we would do bits of his neighborhood, his gait as if he were on a shifting stage, trying out versions of himself. Even now there's something vulnerable and exposed about his gestures. That thin stream. The rustling yellow grass. The little we leave behind, Stevens says, sticks and mud, a few words between friends. But how they cry out, how they draw the eye in when we are no more. End of the day, the two of us walking his neighborhood, exaggeratedly careful about the footing, stealing glances up as the shadows deepen, the angled rooflines the next street over suddenly alive, "smeared with the gold of the opulent sun."

Left church early to drive to Richmond for Abby's first birthday. Clouds tall and distinct this side of the Blue Ridge, lower and dense and rainlike when we passed over. How often I've noticed this between the two valleys—clouds carded and squeezed and extruded on one side of this great rib of mountains, gone on the other. Thomas Traherne sees creation as a kind of theater of desire—God's restless wanting endlessly displayed, infinitely reaching towards us. "You must want like a God that you may be satisfied like God," he writes. What would be the shape of that? I've been reading his *Centuries*, paragraph-length reflections on creation and, I suppose you would say, joy, gathered into sets of one hundred, discovered in manuscript form in a wheelbarrow outside a London bookstore in 1896, more than two hundred years after his death. The clouds: endlessly displayed and just as endlessly let go, as if the wanting behind them were more important than the thing itself, however intensely seen and loved. As if desire were quietly massing on the horizon and drawing the heart out to it, as if desire were our true home.

Perhaps it looks like this. Laura and I hiked to McAfee's Knob today. Eight miles, a tough climb, harder on the way down. Occasional sightings of other hikers on the switchbacks, both of us wondering how to judge someone else's pain, how one would even begin to take that in. Crazy wind on top. We saw a hiker's hammock, strung between trees, out on the knob itself, empty and rocking in the wind. Late at night now, legs still aching, thinking of that hiker, held and shaken in the dark. Alone out there in the wind's longing, pressed into its shape and sensing that whatever passes for speech must be speech for him and him alone. Oddly though, it's the empty hammock I see, twisting in the dark, when I try and squint my eyes to imagine him. As if I can't yet, from here, put myself entirely in his place, can't bear up under what holds him down, the empty hammock nobody's home, twisting and wrapping around itself.

Sunday night, falling asleep, I feel the lightest of hands on my shoulders. It's not Laura, although the pressure is like the way she often touches me as we drift off. It might be the moon, full tonight, although what the moon would want to reassure me about I can't say. Walking this afternoon, we stopped at a silvery stump on a low bank usually under water. The tree must have toppled in years ago when beavers first dammed the creek, the top of the stump chain sawed smooth, four or five silver roots lifted free of the ground, gripping the air, one thumb still attached to the drying mud. Imagine the moon tonight on the back of that hand. "He does not see the moon," Bishop writes of the ordinary man she begins her poem with. "He observes only her vast properties, / feeling the queer light on his hands, neither warm nor cold." I wonder though. He is not the strange, light-drawn figure she imagines climbing tall buildings toward the small hole opened in the sky and the radiance just beyond it, and yet, the rest of the city asleep or underground, he is the one still out here, the only one the silky moon can find tonight to speak to.

The sharp, aching loneliness of these October trees, 5:00, end of the day, lit from the west. Long shadows, above them reds and yellows and various greens, darker and dominating. I spoke about the passage in Mark 8 today where Jesus heals a blind man by touching his eyes twice. "Do you see anything," he asks the first time. The man looks up, into a flood of sensation: "Men, but they look like trees walking," he says, shifting planes of shadow and stride having filled the place of the familiar. He touches him again and his sight is restored. But imagine the moment between—leaning forward, perhaps covering his eyes to gather himself and see in his mind the winking light of the trees. I remember, when I began to find myself in college, listening to Jack open up a text and touch it to our eyes, simply by describing what he was seeing. And then a pause—his eyes somewhere else, a tree at the window—seemingly waiting for us to catch up. Two days ago I visited him and Katherine in Lewisburg. He was no longer able to follow the turns of our conversation, but he asked about my mother and twice broke in: "Did you see her picture?" and "a thing and its glory." I wish I had asked about that. It was as if he had stepped aside from the conversation, not so much to wait for us but to savor something that had finally come undone there, gathering himself as the light darkened and drained away, day's burden down, moving freely across the courtyard to join us.

Layers of yellow in the trees out back this afternoon, their bottoms already in shadow where the woods draw down to the stream, their tops, at eye level from where I sit, alive in the sun, flat and then alive again as clouds race overhead. I'm trying to work out a sense of perspective. A splash of red, then what might be ten or twelve layers of yellow and yellow-green moving away from me, cut by two or three dead branches angling across the layers and opening up the stage. Birds catch the light like drops of water in your hair as you walked from the shower to the bed. Was that a dream? One's "innermost chambers" house a "burning bush," if one could but see, writes the painter Makoto Fujimura. I'm reminded of the layers of pigment filtered through gold in his show last year, the eye longing to pick a way down that darkening path. I'm not sure how much time has passed. I'm still in my chair, watching the glistening light slide away, down through the wall of windows. Somewhere beyond me, part of me has come undone, the part that is wholly fire.

Abby's babble yesterday as we walked up to the falls, more rhythm than words, some lost song fading in and out again against the rocks, tumbling to mist in the stream below. She's on her father's back. I'm behind, adjusting my steps, keeping an eye on the way her left hand rubs itself in tight spaces against rocks and trees, her right hand a dangling rhododendron leaf. Three days ago I'd been walking with a friend who had broken an arm badly at the gym. When they went to set it, he flat lined for almost two and a half minutes, the anesthesia and shock having stopped his heart. When they revived him, the life flooding back caused his heart to swell—broke it, essentially, or so the condition's name suggested—and he wanted to talk about the new sense of himself he'd fallen into. A sort of conversion, but to what he didn't know. No Damascus road, no blinding light. It was ten days since the accident and something he couldn't name had untied itself in him. When my brother died, I lost almost all of the week before, but this was a different sort of emptiness. It was like waiting for something new to be born, he said—temporarily full of wonder at how easily the old words had disappeared, the broken arm tightly bound under his shrugged on coat, me walking beside him, trying to figure out how much space to leave. On our way home, I found myself edging out into the street as if to form a barrier against the afternoon traffic. How much room does a broken heart need to find its way back to itself? What would that new song be like? And what might it cost to put yourself near enough to hear it?

Spending the weekend in Burlington with my siblings and their spouses and Mom and Dad. Hiking today along the Haw River. Yellowing woods in the direct afternoon sunlight. You can see along the river where last month's high water, after Hurricane Matthew, had passed. Leaves jammed high in trees, pieces of torn plastic stranded five or six feet above the water's level today, debris everywhere where the water had receded. We snake up and down the low hills in ones and twos, pausing at the river, not saying much, then starting up again, each of us working our way up to Dad and then falling away again to open a space for the others. The beauty of it all. Roger Lundin died a year ago today. He had invited me out to Wheaton that October to give a few talks and share a class on Dickinson. By the time of my visit, his health had declined, but he rallied and came to two of the classes. They would be the last ones he ever taught. The first, if I remember right, went more or less in a straight line. The second, a week later, was like nothing I had ever experienced before. He wanted to talk about the emptiness after light, in its searing unteachable way, had moved on. Sumptuous destitution, Dickinson called it. Could we understand that, as comfortable and modern as we all were? A pause, and then something inside him broke and he was suddenly a child again, abandoned and alone. Tears on his face, hands moving on their own. Forgive me. "Infinitude—," he whispered, "Had'st Thou no Face / That I might look on Thee?" I'm not sure how he found his way to her in the dark. There was silence again, and then, the class having apparently ended, we, who "were not the one dead," in ones and twos, pressing his hands on the way out, "turned to [our] affairs."

Heavy loud wind for a second day. There are enough leaves still left in the oaks that it roars as it approaches and then, after a pause, lifts the leaves I'm trying to rake into a dozen mad streamers away from me. I wonder if you're watching me try to time the pulses and then toss the rake into the mayhem and walk away. After he gave up philosophy and his share of the family fortune, Wittgenstein's sister Hermine turned on him for wasting his life. He replied, "You remind me of somebody who is looking out through a closed window and cannot explain to himself the strange movements of a passer-by." You can't tell what sort of storm is raging out there, he said, or what a struggle it might be to stay on your feet. Some years ago, my father, my mother, and I worked on a book together in which they talked their way through growing up in the Depression. What was your first memory, I would ask. In your mind, go out your front door and turn right. Take me down the road. When I played back the tapes and began to transcribe them, I could hear the difference in their voices— my father's textured and precise, in love with the swelling surfaces of things; my mother's abrupt and resonant, a child left alone in an empty classroom. There was some invisible wind about to drop down on her, still roaring through the trees. We never spoke about it, but I want to say that my hand took something in as it copied out her words and worked them into sentences. "All this and not ordinary," Gertrude Stein wrote in 1914, five years before Wittgenstein failed to explain himself to his sister. She was talking about the way a "single hurt color" can be sensed pressing its way through an arrangement of words, soaking through a tablecloth or scattering a partially raked lawn, leaving to pen and paper the task of shaping voices into a new sort of pattern, "not unordered in not resembling."

I've woken up the past two mornings with vertigo, the room sliding away as I try to get my legs under me in the dark. It settles down during the day, but when I walk or run, I feel as if I'm always two feet in front of myself, stumbling toward something I can never quite reach. Extraordinary browns this year, late in the leaf-fall, the yellows gone, browns shading bronze and red as the sun picks out something we might like and raises it to our eyes. "Desire satisfied is a Tree of Life," Traherne writes. I think he must mean this bronzed longing I can't get enough of at the edge of our property or down the mountain heading for work. *The Tree of Life*—Terrence Malick used that as well as a title for a film I love. I remember, the first time I saw it, getting caught up in a friend's frustration at its seemingly unending answer to the central figure's desperate question about how his mother survived his brother's death, the film abruptly shifting from family life in Texas to a grand unfurling of cosmic light, the light's argument infinitely sustained, pulsing and condensing and—I don't know how else to say this—reaching out toward us in the dark. My friend shifted his feet and looked around. A few people got up and left. Afterwards, we pretended to find it pretentious, but I think now we were overwhelmed at how close it had come, at the longing it had set in motion but refused, finally, to draw to a close or satisfy. As if it had turned to each of us and asked, "Where were you when I laid the foundations of the earth.... When the morning stars sang together, and all the sons of God shouted for joy?" And what could I say? It was all I could do to stand and walk, steadying myself on the backs of seats as I made my way to the doors.

34 degrees and cold rain as I walk to the top of Brush Mountain. Clouds moving through the bare trees, plumes of smoke from chimneys. The steady sound of rain against the not-yet-compressed layers of leaves on the ground, the sound singular and amplified and—could this be the right word?—lonely. The secret is almost too plain and I stop several times, wondering if anyone else has noticed. It's as if in a crowded room a vial of ointment had been spilled—poured out, rather, on the calmly consenting woods, the rain so entranced that nothing could stand in its way as it unbound its hair and fell to its knees. How lonely and how strange, how utterly unguarded. Do you remember the little world Ann and Katie built out of bits of trash on the Outer Banks, years ago? The two of us peering in, under the dripping deck, and then drawing away, probably unnecessarily; each of them so deeply intent at their separate tasks that nothing could have come between them and the worlds they held in their hands.

The low long clouds this morning as the sun rose like a Howard Finster angel cut out of plywood, their whites and grays pulled into flame and gleaming orange and then yellow and then after ten minutes gone. Maybe you've seen them—some of them as much as eight feet long, flat-faced, their wings covered with names and verses, arms out front raising a pole from which plywood banners trail, their visions announced in a child's capital letters. The one this morning had been moving to the east, into the sun, but paused, smiling, for us to take in its flowing robe and darker wings and banners. We never got close enough to read the words. When we had finished putting our book together, my mother one day, out walking, said, "There are things I didn't tell you because they would be lies." Maybe we all trail such scrawled, unreadable banners. It's been cold. In the afternoon, the upper pond was completely frozen, the lower, deeper pond perhaps half way, thin sheets of ice along all the edges and across the coves. If the wind rises tonight, those sheets will break free and be pushed down to one end. And if the temperature drops, those floating panels will be welded together into a single surface by morning, the new ice and the old marbled together into a painstaking cursive you can just make out in the first light.

Quiet walk today, almost silent, alone in a cold, wet wind. I'd expected to hear, at least, the shimmering sound of white oak leaves but the hard wind over the last few days seems to have ripped most of them down. Across the pond, the hollow sound of waves against the new dock. The rumble of gunfire from the shooting range, at least a mile away. We've never actually seen it, but you always know it's there. What my mother hadn't said was both simple and terrible. That she had learned, in her fifties, assembling paperwork for a passport, that her father wasn't her birth father. That she had been born some time before her father married her mother and that the rest of her family—her younger siblings included—had known but not her. I keep thinking of the restored theater we had seen in Stockholm, wooden waves and clouds and mountains on rails, poised to be tugged, rumbling, into place. It was as if the stage she thought she had lived her childhood on wasn't a stage at all, or it wasn't the one she thought. But it was also as if, even as a child, she had heard something in that silence that couldn't be said and had opened herself up to it, giving it a body and a voice. "The singing of the real world," Virginia Woolf called it, under the silence of the world we inhabit.

That singing. I'm outside the house with Isaiah and Caroline, gathering bits of things and making up stuff. I pretend I'm doing it for them. He's three, she's five. When we run, she falls into a full sprint and pulls away from me. He runs the way he talks, arms and legs all over the place, pausing for a moment where the road falls away and then plunging down. Whitman plays a similar sort of game with the child in "Song of Myself" who comes racing up to him with hands full of grass. It's a flag, a handkerchief, a ruined language that no one can read. And then he suddenly pulls away and turns within—"And now it seems to me the beautiful uncut hair of graves."—their beauty having torn open in him some sort of private space. When we get back to the house, we notice that the heart we'd assembled on the sidewalk out of acorns and berries had been accidentally kicked through. Stand here with me, won't you? The children have already moved on. It's somehow more beautiful broken—this torn-through scrawl, its windows open and edges all undone. This emptying vessel, filling with song.

The pond has been freezing and melting for weeks. Walking this afternoon, we weren't sure what we were seeing—in the shallow end, what seemed to be long strands of grass reaching almost to the surface, bent off there and trailing 6-8 inch needle-like segments. I'd woken several times from a dream this morning with the thought of moving through fields of high grass, light overhead as I squeezed my way through. It was something like that, though we were outside of it and somewhat above. We stopped but couldn't tell for sure. You found a rock and tossed it out, and when it tore a hole through the surface everything changed; we were looking at a thin sheet of ice, its just-forming crystalline threads not broken-off blades of grass but the first traces of the invisible taking form. In my dream I was thinking about thinking, about being lost—something I never would have known except for whatever had torn through the nearly invisible structures I was elaborating in my sleep and woken me up. That ragged little hole. That almost casual *plop* of a rock through the ice. A sound we barely registered. Hard to admit that I had turned away from some part of myself because I didn't think to bend down and grab something hard and heave it out there. Shyness is the word I used when I tried to explain to David why I'd been unable to break a decades-long silence between us, but I don't think it's only that. Some reluctance to trust myself to thin ice, to plunge through it, as of course I would, into uncertainty. To wake myself from sleep. But why? What have I got to lose? The rock arcing, the hole about to open. Nothing else would seem to matter.

An almost absent day, sketching long blue shadows across the snow in a notebook at 3:30, the same long shadows hours later from the opposite direction as the moon began to rise. A day spent almost entirely at the window, or so it seemed. The shadows like a half-built hut coming slowly undone as blue sank down to black. "The soul is made for action, and cannot rest till it is employed. Idleness is its rust," Traherne mutters from a dark corner of the room. We did walk, I try to say, but we couldn't make anything out of it. It was very cold. The pond had frozen except for three round holes near the middle. They were like buttons. The ice itself was a gloppy gray, having taken in five inches of new snow just as it covered itself over. Think of layered, under-lit evening clouds, or the graying light thickened by cold. The world wasn't just idle, it was no world at all. There was nothing moving over the face of its waters, nothing one could imagine which didn't immediately turn away from words. Even the voice of creation was inward and away.

When my student Graham came into my office and told me he had finally faced in himself the shame we all haul about from our childhoods, he was still carrying around the discarded brake shoe he had found along a set of railroad tracks to remind himself. Why don't you leave it here, I said, and there it sits, four or five years after our conversation. I'm not sure why I haven't been able to move it or toss it out. It was as if I'd seen in him one of the broken forms desire takes but had set it aside, unsure what to do next. We could go there and I could show you. In *The Tree of Life*, as Jack is thinking back on the loss of his brother and the emptying out of the world that followed, he asks, in voiceover, "How did she bear it?," meaning his mother. The camera turns to his mother and father on the day they got the news. They are alone—Jack and his brother are grown and would have been long out of the house by then—and they seem dazed, underwater. His mother stares out a window, his father closes the piano as if for the last time. At some point, you realize we are watching them from over Jack's shoulder, but it's an older Jack, perhaps the same age as they are now. The scene must be a reflection on what it would take to make something out of her pain. Jack walks across the room and touches her hair—she doesn't respond, of course; he's not there—and says, quietly, "Mother." He's staging the scene internally, lifting the weight along with her and allowing himself to know and feel and grow silent. Perhaps shaking out of God a nearly impenetrable answer. But he had to go there. He had to imagine the very texture of her hair and the feel of it against his hand. He had to break, himself, in order to follow her back to life.

Last night, the two of us in a terrible storm, picking our way over Fancy Gap on the road back from Greensboro. We'd been to see David's play and I was trying to describe what it had been like to sit with him in the dark as that love between the two boys unfolded and broke and reformed, wanting and yearning shifting between the two figures and then the third like songs we all knew from camp, songs you surely knew better than I did. Driving and trying to sort out those years when he and I first knew each other, the life inside that had stirred in me that I still associate with him though I hadn't told him so for forty years. How I had turned away, as if I knew I wasn't able to handle then those worlds opening up and the demands they seemed to make. How it felt like a betrayal. How I was, not for the first time, trying to return to those moments and make them fall out differently, or at the very least see them more clearly. I needed you there to draw me out, listening as I had listened, hours before. I think now I couldn't imagine there was enough of myself to share—or that I feared that was so. By that point, we were far from the play, though I was fingering parts of it that had come undone and still clung to me as the rain broke across the car. And now, this morning, reading Traherne again on God's aching communication of himself, splintering in a thousand shapes and directions across the world's stage. David's play ended with an out of sequence swoop back to the beginning, the two boys boys again but changed, as if it were possible to return to the past, to hold both it and its complications and unfoldings together in one hand. To look up, after all those years, invisible audience, and if you get the music right, to touch that wanting, to not hold tight while not letting go.

Walking alone at the pond about 3:30, cold, snow in the air, the leaves on the ground an infinite number of intersecting planes, their brown tinged with white, leading the eye to open space far back in the trees. The silence opening up as well—a slight breeze through the cattails, under it the sound of water lapping and nuzzling, distant traffic in shifting pitches and colors, guns, singly or in cascading chains, a plane overhead, a high pulsing whine I can't locate, like crickets or tree frogs in another season. Traherne describes the air as "a penetrable body," by which he must mean this overfilled, resonant quickening. How deep you could look into such beauty, how long you could spend. By the time I get back to the house, heavy snow is falling, thickening the air. The lines of trees are distinguishable for a few minutes against the white background but the space they mark quickly collapses, the white background sweeping forward, the cross-hatched trees and branches darker against the white for a moment and then swept away in a gray-blue blankness. All of it gone. Perhaps this is what Stevens meant, though in lines I've never really understood, that while "Beauty is momentary in the mind," "in the flesh it is immortal." The flesh of the world, the snow-touched, penetrable air.

Twenty turkeys, moving across the back yard this afternoon, blending into each other and the dark, sun-patched woods. Their heads, one after another, momentarily lift and peer out, their shifting brown bodies drifting down and away from me. It's impossible to hold them all in your eyes—even now the head of the conga line has vanished in the woods' low growth. You could film them, I suppose, but even that wouldn't do them justice. This might work though. I've been thinking lately of the famous, twelve-frame running man sequence Eadweard Muybridge created in the late 19th century. Perhaps you've seen them—twelve slightly comic, deeply serious photographs of a nude man running, viewed from the side. Muybridge's stop-motion photographs let us see what had been almost invisible: the left foot about to plant, the right arm high and forward; that arm swinging lower and back, the right foot lifting, both feet floating for an uncanny moment, and then the right foot planting; the right hand now moving forward again and the left foot up and out and ready to plant. The head never moves while the rest of the body almost unnaturally springs and gathers and floats, a grid of twelve takes against a dark background. It's one of the most beautiful things I've ever seen, the gap between each photograph making the resistance the body is working against visible—as if beginning again, week after week, might let us hear the silence the urgent body and the almost stilled mind press into and draw a world out of.

These Sundays, carved out of ordinary time. I've been waking an hour or so early—4:30 or 4:45—for the past week. Completely alert, nothing anymore to fear. Full moon through the window; the night, ripped by a crazy, howling wind, almost over. The half-seen figures prompted by Laura's struggles at work now quieted, exhausted. I begin, in my mind, gathering fragments—twigs, branches, bits of sentences—wanting to make a shape. I feel as if I can't move, as I'm waiting for something to come and release me, to call my name in the dark. As if, a friend writes, we're excavating the ruin of our days, sifting through its pieces. The moon and stars very clear. In Mexico once, Laura and I stopped to swim in a cenote, a great sinkhole, partly filled with water. Bottomless, the driver said, and walked off to smoke. Maybe fifty steps down to the water, carved out of rock. A ledge. The dark surface half in and out of sunlight. Ferns hanging down, a steady patter of drips. We swam to opposite walls and then met in the middle. I remember sliding under the surface and pushing down hard in the dark. Then again, as deep as I dared, and waiting, gathering myself before pushing back up to the surface, only to feel you dropping down, joining me there, brushing the length of my body—the two of us undone together until we rose, as we all must, blinking in the glinting air.

Laura left this morning for five days, in a stab of sunrise. 5:00 now, walking in shadow, a silvery light on the trees above me and across the pond on the hills. All day I've been fumbling at the edges of a loneliness so deep it scares me. On Friday, I visited a friend in the hospital. She's almost blind and had fallen. As I helped her eat—I was glad for something to do, I didn't want to stare—she described the route that had brought her there, to that bed, this room. I know it doesn't seem possible, she said, I must have been hallucinating, but the details are so clear I can feel them still, as if a few half-dreamed images were all she had been given to make her way back to life, peering back at some version of herself, poised there still between light and paint, or shadows and the silvery hills. She was almost radiant in her dismissal of that impossible accounting, in the grip of something so compelling there would be no unseeing it. Or so it had seemed. It's what I feel now, staring into myself, walking around, glad for something to do with my body, the rest of me, invisible audience, waiting to be called there too.

Woke Sunday with vertigo again, grabbing walls and chairs as I stumbled around in the dark, weaving up the driveway thirty minutes later to get the paper, whatever was off in my inner ear finally reducing itself to a slight drift to the right as we walked around the pond later that afternoon. Sick to my stomach Monday night and now, ten minutes into my Tuesday class, I've had to stop, walk out into the hall, and sit against a wall to gather myself. I can feel my students' eyes at first, but the pressure against my back frees me somehow, sitting in the hall as if waiting for someone to squat down beside me and ask what I had seen. When we were nine and ten, my brother and I would crawl through the storm drain that ran at the edge of our property, one behind the other in the dark. Spider webs and mud, sudden damp smells, intersections where we'd pause and back our way out, returning the next day and pushing on through, picking one way or another. We'd take turns leading, on forearms and knees, blind, mapping that space in the dark, working it out inwardly. A kind of shared, silent dream. I think I could still make my way through that maze today, the route folded away in my head. When we finally reached the road—after how many tries?—one of us squeezed all the way into that open space, crossways, back against the wall, while the other worked his head up to the other's lap, both of us staring up through the grate. Clouds racing, sounds of the world returning again, the two of us wildly free under it all, quiet, as if not to give ourselves away. I'm not sure how long I sat there or what I said at first to the class, all of us oddly careful with each other the first few minutes after I returned.

The first, wordless green in the briars this morning stops me dead in my tracks. "Why are you downcast, O my soul," it says. "Why are you in turmoil within me?" I'm not sure. But I'm unable to move, frozen up inside. In Wisconsin, when the ice broke up this time of year, the wind would push the shattered remaining bits into a massive new shoreline along the path I rode to work. I'd stop to take it in, the waves slowly sliding toward me through the shimmering hush, the dark, open lake beyond. At night, just before sleep, I'd find myself back at that shoreline. Come out, the shifting ice would call to me, and I'd stand there for hours, imagining my first steps—the cold shock, gradually regaining my balance, not quite lifting my feet but sliding them through the glistening slush, up and over the waves. "I believe in you, my soul," Whitman wrote, perhaps out of a similar sort of lostness. "I mind how once we lay such a transparent summer morning, / How you settled your head athwart my hips and gently turn'd over upon me"—the memory, tugging at him, calling him out or back. These past few weeks, I've seen those wobbling attempts to walk mirrored in my two youngest grandchildren. As if, all these years later, none of that longing had truly been lost, bits of it gathered up by the March wind and deposited here, all of us hearing the same cry in the same cold wind—come out, come away, let go.

Extraordinary moment, earlier in the week. My right eye had suddenly come undone—what seemed like bolts of lightning began rippling down one side of it, the light show when I walked across a dark parking lot almost continuous. I went to the eye doctor who described it as posterior vitreous detachment—the vitreous gel pulling away from the back of the eye, tugging at the retinal nerve cells and sending signals the brain was taking in as light. Age, I suppose. He probed the eye with a bright, stabbing light, and I suddenly saw a vast field stretching out before me—an empty yellow-brown desert; dried up, interwoven stream beds laced one to the next across branching, angled ridges. I couldn't breathe. It was as if I had suddenly glimpsed some inner blankness I'd never been able to open myself up to before. It lasted for four or five seconds and then faded. Blood vessels laced across the retina, the doctor explained when I jerked my head back and looked around the darkened room—always there but ignored by the brain, their shadows thrown a new way against the back wall of the retina by his probing light and so momentarily visible, momentarily taken in. I'd never seen anything as beautiful or as terrible. Now, in a new morning's dark, the lightning flashes have begun again, though not as intensely as before. It's as if, in a darkened room, a blind were shifting in the faintest of breezes and, just for a moment and then again, the moon outside had pushed its way through. You could go there, I thought. You really could. The blind flapping and flapping in some insistent inner breeze.

Jack Wheatcroft died last Tuesday—a friend from the school called me. I've been thinking about him all week, how listening to him make his way through books drew me toward a part of myself I didn't know what to do with. Loneliness was the word I used for it then, or lostness. I would walk out at night, through town, to the bridge over the Susquehanna, and stare down. Hisses and sighs, all that energy sliding under me in the dark, calling me somewhere else. I thought I was thinking about dying, but I think now it was something else. Deep within us is a river, under it all, where everything comes undone. Longing starts there, and wanting, murmuring and clucking, endlessly braiding over itself in the dark. Call it the soul, this endless longing and wanting. I don't think, anymore, it matters what we call it—this field folded away in thought. I remember too that I was stumbling toward faith at the time, thinking I was turning away from that dark river rather than, as it seems now, embracing it. Another way my doctor tried to describe what was going on with my eye was a boat on a lake tied loosely to a dock. Imagine a wind coming up, storm clouds. Each time the boat pulled away from the dock and the rope tightened, that would be the gel tugging at the retina, triggering those flashes of light. The smallest thing—tugs in the dark, the piling up clouds. Calling me out there, shifting the blinds, that river of wanting making its way below me the dark.

Waiting. It must be 4 AM or so, but I don't want to look at the clock. For the last hour I've felt as if I were taking dictation. A phrase would come into my head, and I'd consider it for a moment, say it back to myself, and then drop back almost to sleep, waiting on the next tug. I imagine this is how the five pairs of geese I've seen nesting at the pond sleep—their heads turned back into themselves, the male floating just offshore, jostled by anything that ventures near. I want to show Laura those nests when we walk this afternoon. It's too early to do anything with these words except turn them around in my head and wait. In my first two years of high school I worked summers on my grandfather's and uncle's dairy farms. I was almost entirely alone and on Sundays, when they were both sleeping, I'd go on long walks through the fields, dirt lanes taking me from one to the next, sometimes up a rise, sometimes down along a creek. It felt something like this—as if I were meeting some part of me that wasn't me yet. I remember loving the way one field would back up against another— my uncle was buying up land those summers—and having to sometimes work my way through brush or fence lines to keep the conversation going. I'd circle and drift for miles. It seemed like a form of prayer, if prayer were waiting and considering and taking the world slowly in rather than the fretful scratching at fears I often fall into. I hated to go to sleep those summers, as tired as I always was. I knew that as soon as my head touched the pillow someone would be shaking me awake to start all over again. Funny to think of that now, my nights so long and open, the gentlest of motions jostling one door open after another.

Frightening moment last night when, out of a light sleep, my eye exploded in a field of white followed, two or three seconds later, by a clap of thunder. I was relieved when the thunder came—I was sure the broken hut of my eye had given way and I was taking in, all at once, what had been, until then, sifting in through the blinds. But how beautiful those two or three seconds before I realized it was lightning, the receding light etching the dark room with pockets of a black so deep and textured you could imagine looking down into it forever. "I must lead you out of this, into another world, to learn your wants," a voice says in Traherne. What a strange business. A year or two after the storm drain obsession, my brother and I fell deeply in love with a tree. I don't know how else to say this. We named it. We circled it all day long, every day, waiting for the bus in its lower branches, racing to fit ourselves back into the clouds when school was finally over and we spilled off the bus and climbed it again. It was just across the street. Our Tree of Life, but even Traherne remarks on the strange way wanting underwrites the having—the room aflame with it, as if wanting were a fountain that never exhausted itself, as if wanting were itself the thing sought, the treasure we could all but take in our hands there, resting our weight on the swaying, uppermost branches.

Laura and I, walking the pond Sunday afternoon with Alli, Matt, and Abby. They learned on Thursday that she had lost her baby's heartbeat. We've done this walk since Alli was a small child and we hoped it might order our feelings and give us a way to talk, but something would not give way, insects whirling, an odd pewter sheen on the water. "The World that thou has opened / Shuts for thee," Dickinson wrote, across the meadow, to her sister-in-law Sue. "But not alone, / We all have followed thee." That's the problem, I think—how to follow her into this shut world. Two nights ago, when she called with the news, I felt as if I were outside my body, piecing together from Laura's side of the conversation what must have happened. I feel like that now, as if I were lagging behind the group and can't keep up, can't find a way in. As if the pond were a stage and I was holding myself back in the wings. I can feel myself drifting away. "Awe is the first Hand that is held to us [there]," Dickinson writes in the same letter, and maybe that's it. That this uncertain drift—the self blank and wordless and increasingly alone—isn't alone at all. Awe is waiting for us there, holding out its hand and inviting us to wander and listen and caress. It pauses itself to find the words. It reaches out for a grieving mother's hair.

Easter, the shootings at Virginia Tech ten years ago today. We've driven part way up John's Mountain to where the Appalachian Trail crosses it and then hiked north to Kelly Knob, a steep half mile and then easier going along the ridge. A hawk over us at the knob, the hills around campus in the hazy distance. Improvised fireplace behind us, leafless trees below, virtually no green up here at all, in fact. The barest of stage sets. We imagine being here at night, the wind whipping, trying to get a fix on distant, flickering lights. It's as if we are drifting on a thermal ten years in the making and don't have the eyes to make out anything below us, though surely something in the wind had called out to us as it swept us up to this height. There's nothing to say. What's down there seems as settled and fixed as these worn away hills. A through hiker passes behind us, pauses, and then exits stage left. We go too, though we turn away from him and make our way back down the way we came. And then—I'm not sure who saw it first—but as we picked our way down the trail and then the rest of the way down to the valley, the green came back—and not only green but redbud, dogwood, cherry, newly-opened fields and calves alongside mothers. It was as if a blind had shifted, as if the mountain itself had split open along one side and the invisible world all of this was resting upon had risen up to meet us. Now I can't drive slowly enough. None of this is settled, everything is unfolding and opening up from within, some tucked-away stream carving away at us under a just about to crumble bank.

Pelting rain all the way down to Abingdon and then continuing through the play. You could hear it on the roof. Still pounding as we dash for our car and make our way out of town. Our friend Loren is driving. Coming down a slight dip we slow and then stop. A creek has overflowed its culvert and is spreading across the road. We don't really know how deep it is, though the disappearing tail lights of a car maybe twenty seconds ahead of us and what we thought we saw as it passed through lets us guess. This seems more real than the silly play. We nod and slowly move forward, the water up around the doors, the car rocking a little, and then we're through. Perhaps it was foolish. In twenty minutes it surely would have been. I think we would have turned around then and tried another way, but honestly I'm not sure. This lonely river calling me, this flood of yearning—how do you know when it becomes too much? My mother's family used horses to put up hay. After it had been cut and raked and dried, they loaded it on wagons. It was her job to ride up top and build the load. It was no simple thing—storm clouds would pile up most afternoons, and the fields were anything but level. The load might shift and come apart and you'd be the one they'd blame. I could hear that in her voice as we eased our way down into her past and began to build our book there. What if there were no bottom? Sometimes, without meaning to, someone would throw a snake up with the hay and you'd have to manage, she said. You would. I wonder if you're imagining it now—a quick flash, something rising and turning in the air, the young girl very still, her eyes reaching for what she can't turn away from, just before it hits and disappears.

Walking around the pond, early evening, after the long drive back from Annapolis, rooting ourselves in the world we know. Back at the house and a call from Matt in the ER where he had taken Alli with complications from the miscarriage. We've had three calls since then, each of them, like the first, broken off when a doctor or nurse comes with more information, or a question, or to start a procedure. It's 9:00 now and our nerves are jangled. The silence between calls is a torment—there's nothing we can do from this distance. It eats away at us. It refuses to be contained. I want to say that something in the silence calls us to itself, but I can't. I won't. Each time the phone rings, the voice behind it comes undone. It's as if silence were reaching out a hand but neither of us were strong enough to take it. Who would have thought it could stoop this low and kneel and speak? The wind rising, boats bumping against the dock. It's come all this way for us, but we're not ready to go out with it, not yet.

Sunday night bonfire with friends. The host tells a story about a drop-in visit from someone who had been at a massive party at this house years before, apparently involving a water slide from a second-story window. I'm not sure if I have the details right—we're all shifting about with the smoke, I'm coughing with what I guess are allergies, and it's hard to hear. Our stories spin off of each other like the line of Lady's Slippers Laura and I saw arcing off the trail this afternoon, pulling us away from wherever it was we had been heading. One of us recounts a dream—she had come to in the middle of a vast, blue lake. She could see for miles. White clouds reflected in the water, patches of sunlight rising up and sliding away as far as she could see in any direction. And a feeling of peace, a vast blue feeling of peace. We wait for more, and when she can't go on, someone says, "You were remembering your own birth." No reply, and the stories begin again, the smoke moving us around the circle in different pairings and groups, as if it were trying to work something out. We'll never get it out of our clothes. I keep coming back to my mother's lonely childhood. Surely I grew up in its shade, but it's hard to look at directly. It was not death, or frost, or night, Dickinson writes of a similar inner blankness, but it "tasted like them all," her poem a trickling stream of *likes* and *as ifs* entertained and then set aside, the poem finally coming to rest at something "Stopless—cool"—as if that vast blue lake were under all our stories, as if the shifting smoke of longing, in moving us about and never letting us settle, had been all along bringing us to this other place, where wanting was itself a home, where since no one was expected anyone could appear.

Had to stop twice on the walk around the pond today and now, as if at the ocean on the edge of a storm, my fever is coming on in waves, rising, twice my size, pushed by the wind all the way up to the dunes and then drawing back, under a darkening sky. My fingers and joints are hollowed out and aching. I can't stop coughing. Each wave scrapes a little more of me away, and it would seem to be only a matter of time before a final one rises up and rushes in, emptying me and taking my body for its own. I'm OK with that. There's no real reason to fight it. One of the things I love about Malick's *Thin Red Line* is its central, framing voice, that of a nameless soldier who we see only once or twice, frightened and babbling, trying to right himself as they move toward the battle and then again as they move away, the sea rising and lowering beneath them. The movie seems to rise out of some empty space inside him—a grave, formal voice, not his at all; a silent, inward voice, shattered and re-made, intimate, open-eyed at the beauty and terror around him. We lose him in the crowd as the troop transport pulls away from the island, but his voice kneels down beside us for a moment: "Is this darkness in you too? Have you passed through this night?" And then it moves on, though we can still make it out, beside us in the dark. It sounds almost like a prayer, if prayer were what remained after everything else had been stripped away. Engines roaring, the island receding, speaking to what called out to him from within: "Let me be in you now. Look out through my eyes. Look out at the things you made."

I need to tell you something. When I stayed home from church this morning, it wasn't just that I was still weak from the pneumonia, though getting that cough and fever diagnosed last week had set me back—just having a name for the thing turned my body against itself in a determinedly focused way. No, the antibiotics had kicked in enough for me to go out. I think I just wanted to be alone and stare out the back windows. Yesterday, I had noticed that the new green had almost completely closed the house in, and I think I wanted to sink all the way in and leave myself behind. Leaves moving, a blue black sky through breaks in the trees, and then a tapping against the bedroom window. A fluttery tapping, over and over, too insistently regular to be the redbud I'd carelessly let grow up against the window. It was a male bluebird—I got up to look, fluttered my arms in response to try to startle him—attacking his own reflection in the glass, pushing off the redbud and holding himself midair, beating what he saw there with his wings, defending his territory against some equally aggressive rival. (We'd been so pleased a few weeks back when a pair of bluebirds had returned to the house we'd hung at the edge of woods near our bedroom.) It went on for hours. Eventually he grew so tired he simply perched on the sill, lifting himself up only a few inches at a time to beat against himself. I kept coming back to look, something exhausting itself in me as well. That repeated, demented tapping—it made me want to swear off wanting. The smallness of it all. As if for all their beauty, I was only seeing versions of myself in each of these gatherings, and why bother? I was too ashamed when you got home to say anything, but now I think I can. We've been walking here for fifteen years and we've never seen the flame azaleas this thick—this orange, 20-25 thickets of it running down the trail beside us and then off and up a hollow. As if something, in its passing, had set the responding woods aflame with desire and we could still make out its track. Something larger and more beautiful, something uncontrollable. As if, yes, there was something small and self-absorbed in our wanting, but there was also this and it was unending.

Late afternoon, you're settled on the couch quilting, finishing a piece begun eighty years ago by your great grandmother. You've been at it, off and on, for a year and this is the last big push. The fabric bunches at your lap and spills over your knees to the floor. Your face has that sad, considering look it takes on when you concentrate. Lit from within. We saw just that look in one of the Lady and the Unicorn tapestries at the Cluny last summer. Do you remember? She was seated, back straight, in almost exactly this pose, the fabric of her long, layered dress falling in folds to the stylized meadow floor. The unicorn was kneeling at her feet, resting his front legs in her lap. The piece was over 500 years old, beautifully preserved, and, though deeply strange, in the simplicity of its gestures clearly designed to be understood. She would be the soul, I think. He would be the beloved, Christ perhaps. She is gazing down at him. He is looking, not at her exactly, but at the mirror she holds in her right hand, which reflects his face. A floating island of green supports their feet in a tangle of wild flowers and small gazing animals. And there is the look on her face—beautiful, wounded, adored. In looking down at him and at the world he has poured out at her feet, in the almost hidden flicker of arousal there on her face, she is taking in his improbable presence and mirroring it back, the fantastically improvised world about them similarly aflame with desire. Why that sadness, I wonder. It's as if there were something beyond her comprehension in the broken open space his beauty has led her to, just visible in the way her mouth falls open when she's not aware she's being seen. I saw that in you today when we were walking, both of us pausing at the place on the trail where two or three fans of debris had washed across it, me poking through the folds the twigs and leaves and debris had fallen into, you trying to take in what had to have been behind it all, something that had gathered itself overnight and then broken away, tearing its way down the hill toward this mille-fleur island of green.

Looking at an extraordinary photo Matt and Alli just sent—Abby in the early morning sun, sideways to it, looking down her right shoulder and arm at her shadow stretching twice her length across a broken-tiled floor. The camera above her, looking down along with her at the sharply-focused figure. We can't see her eyes but we know exactly what she is looking at. It's as if she has edged up beside a cliff, her left arm stretching back and out of the photo for balance. She's thinking about how much weight this thin plank might bear, utterly at home with how little we know about those mysterious depths each moment is balanced on. I wouldn't be surprised to see her kneel down and lay her entire body across the thin black seam, like a tightrope walker at home between two towers. There's a picture of my mother at age eight or so, squinting into the morning sun, the world seemingly more substantial but with this same long shadow stretching behind her. She's looking out at us at an angle. She's twice the size of her brother and sister and clearly knows something they don't. Do you see her face? Any moment now, we expect her to turn and take those two by the hand, venturing out, across their shadows, on that secret world, however uncertain their first steps might be.

We're halfway up the wall above the falls and stop for a last look. Water droplets in the air, the sun lifting everything up into itself. We're with old friends we haven't seen in twenty years and we're a little lost, all of us trying too hard to make something out of the chain of events that had suddenly brought us together. This is our woods, our favorite trail up to the falls, but we've been acting like tour guides—the slope Hugo had torn through and clear cut a decade ago, the new walkway placed after a terrible spring flood, tiny butterflies that look like violets. It's as if a storm had touched down once and then moved on, leaving only well-meaning behind. We can't get the rhythm right. A father drowned in the pool below us last year when he went in after his son who had gotten caught up in the fall's currents, I say. It was near that rock ledge—you can see how it could have happened, but it still doesn't make sense, not in these rising columns of light and mist, the echoing shouts of other men's children wildly leaping in. Laura has picked up the Finnish lilt in Tuula's voice. I can hear them on the switchback above as they start up again. Tuula's sentences stream out of her in long exuberant plumes of sound, lifting on some inner rise of thought and then plowing to a halt, waiting for Laura to supply the English word. They work almost seamlessly together. Veijo's hanging back with me, I realize, so that he doesn't pull too far ahead and separate us again. Light, shadow, these tiny shifting adjustments, each of us reaching out for the other, plunging under without a thought as to who else might be watching, who might stand ready to follow us in.

A boy at the Solstice Festival yesterday—long hair, eyes closed, his hands up and down in the air in front of him as if he were riding a pair of thermals. As if—we're at the edge of the crowd watching, the crowd swallowing him up and then giving him back again—as if he's on some sort of stage, watching the band in front of him. They're only marginally good. He could have been my student, but he wasn't. He could have been me. "A glimpse through an interstice caught," writes Whitman, of himself and a youth he loves, in a corner of a crowded bar room, amidst the coming and going, slightly set apart, "speaking little, perhaps not a word." What sort of longing, standing there at that open window, could have broken him free from himself like that? What sort of beauty? The boy's palms lift, then turn on their sides, then lift or drop again, stair stepping up and down from one level to the next as if tracing out the threads of an invisible conversation. Laura catches me at night doing something similar with my hands when I'm waiting for her in bed. It has to do with an invisible pressure, I think, with feeling my way toward something that will press back. I've been thinking about that boy for the last hour in the dark. Not him, exactly, but the figure his hands were tracing. It's almost 5 AM now. I've been rising, turning on the light, and writing—scribbling a few words and then laying back again in the dark and waiting. Up and down. Whatever it is, it has called me out of myself, giving itself over in glimpses. The blind swings and then settles back, again and again, whatever is waiting there on the other side almost willing to declare itself. Almost.

The way my mother's voice, sometimes, seems to hang in the air—I thought of that this afternoon, walking under banks of rhododendron spilling down the hillsides. We're 3-4 days short of the peak but these are the days I love, the blooms on the outside edges fully out but at least twice that many, further back, still swelling their way through pale green buds or setting out first, tentative florets, their pink edges more intense than the pink of the full blossoms. "Pinched-out ifs of color," Williams would say, before the full song was ready or able to sing itself. Set apart—these *ifs* or *as ifs*—a way of saying just short of fullness, inhabiting that space as if we were actually free and at rest there but with a catch in the voice just this side of having. My mother has been painting for about ten years, copies of photos, exquisitely and painstakingly done. She has hung them on the walls of their house in clusters and knots of color, three or four deep sometimes—dunes, barns, a mill, arches in the desert, the rocky rise to a lighthouse. A single flower, close up. No people. They read like probes or pauses to get her bearings, welling up from the white space around them, floating on it, as if loneliness itself had found a voice and— the paintings swept up into gatherings almost totally free of any worry about order or scale—it was unbound by anything that had come before.

Southern Shores, walking the beach at night with Laura and Ann, just enough light to make out crabs swarming at our feet and veering away. My sore knee is slowing us down, so I let them go and turn for home. Low waves to my left, maybe a four-foot swell, breaking and sliding in, hushing whatever it is I've been carrying inside. The waves lift and stiffen, and, just as they bend toward breaking, offer the moon an angled surface which it rips a fiery seam across, twenty or thirty feet long. Over and over—the waves rise, catch the light, and then break, their fire fanning out across the beach. This is not unlike the pieces of writing that have been coming to me in the dark or that shifting column of light, Sunday after Sunday, slipping momentarily open when I angle my face just the right way toward it. "At Midnight—I am yet a Maid—," Dickinson writes, eyes on the seam of light under her bedroom door, listening to steps on the stairs. "How short it takes to make it Bride." She rises, her face unreadable in the dark. The steps pause, the door slowly opens, and then she knows—"Master—I've seen the Face—before." But where? Perhaps not only in those flashes of light, I think, but perhaps also in that space between the waves, in the slowly swelling dark. Perhaps more so. The beloved's face held open for her there, his aloneness, his abandonment. That swelling loneliness all desire rises out of.

A day in which nothing seems to have happened—walking the beach early, in the aftermath of a great storm, before driving home. Waves flattened, sky layers of gray, pulled apart just for a moment. A column of light pushing through and then gone. Thought of Nebraska forty-five years ago with John, the two of us having blown the engine of his VW driving too hard all night back to colleges in the east, waiting for three days in the woods behind a gas station in North Platte for an engine. Reading, sleeping, drifting like the high clouds we stared up at, the clothes we'd pulled out to sleep on draped across low bushes to dry out. His story about a secret spot in the woods where he kept cigarettes and a lighter and his favorite shirt to change into on the way to the bus. A faded blue work shirt, not that different from what we all wore, at least that I could see. I might have made that part up—the color of the shirt, how he rubbed the back of his hand across its softening textures. Until just this moment, I'd thought the story was mine, but he must have found that clearing in the woods after I left for college, something in the way his voice sounded in the dark, down behind the gas station, light spilling through two dirty windows, having let me in all those years ago. You have to understand that we never spoke this way. Something undone and lonely in his voice. Maybe it wasn't the hidden away shirt that I've kept and returned to all these years. I doubt my mother really cared about that. Maybe it was the sound of his voice I set aside—undoing itself calling out to me, the strange shape desire takes when it softens and gives way and rises up again. There's a coming undone in God as well, Traherne would say, "the fountain of all His fullness"—the two lit windows above us there like headlights, contending against the night.

Climbing to Mills Lake, Rocky Mountain National Park. We're at Alberta Falls, maybe thirty tumbling feet through a gorge cut by Glacier Creek, about a mile up from the trailhead. People catching their breath or preparing to turn around, most with cell phones out. Below the falls, out of sight of most of the hikers, I see a man on his haunches, out in the middle of the creek, balanced on a flat rock. I'm not sure how he worked his way out there, the falls roaring above us, spray drifting down, the creek falling rapidly away. You'd have to climb down off the trail to see him. He's positioned himself just where the water's undoing begins to gather itself together again. If you look closely, you can see four or five stones he has collected and piled on top of each other. I'm not sure the point, other than carving out a space within all that motion where consciousness might gather itself again. His motions are so slow they seem, in fact, closer to thought than motion, as if, recovering from some sort of trauma, he were isolating a muscle and, ever so slowly, building it back to health. About half an hour after we make it to the lake, a woman crests the boulders where the trail empties out and approaches us, asking if we've seen anyone else up here. Other than the two fly fishermen she can also see, no. She'd become separated from her family and thought surely they'd be waiting here. No. She takes one last look around, asks us to keep an eye out, and plunges back down the trail, presumably to where they might be waiting. It all happens very quickly. Climbing back down to the gorge, we scan faces in each group we meet, trying to find a father and two daughters and, as we promised, pass on word. It all becomes too much—the trail is filled with bodies and shouting, the boundaries between groups blurring and dissolving, the two of us forced to squat down, bad knees and all, and feel around through that rush of water for something solid to lift and hang on to, our hands going numb, our sleeves almost wet to the armpits.

My two brothers-in-law and I are hiking the Perimeter Trail above Ouray, pausing sometimes to figure out our way, our map showing a patchwork of existing trails stitched together to circle the town, 700 feet below us. Cascade Cliff to Cascade Falls, Portland Creek to the Ice Park Trail, the names so ordinary we almost don't take them as applying to these tumbled together foothills and gorges and waterways. At one point an abandoned water tunnel links trail systems on different sides of a stone face, at another, steps cut by miners a century ago do the trick. We're all limping a bit as we finish—not Dickinson's "precarious gait" as she made her way over much vaster bewilderments, but exhausted nonetheless, in an everyday sort of way. If you had been one of those three bronzed women who stopped to help us with our map, you wouldn't have noticed. You probably wouldn't have seen us at all. There came a point where what we each thought of as ourselves gave way and a thin gold line, almost visible as it lengthened and contracted in the late afternoon sun, formed between us. Somebody slipped and we all did, somebody spoke and for just a second you couldn't tell where the voice was coming from. Working our way off the trail and back to town, we can make out the whole route we'd followed. It seems obvious by now, almost logical, and if it weren't for something not quite right in our strides, those awkward links improvised between things might have vanished as well, which would mean, ducking our heads or lowering ourselves down steps cut in stone, losing everything that mattered.

Just returned, after a month away, the last two days in Richmond. Unloaded the car and walked to the pond, just on the edge of dark. Knee a little stiff. Gravel underfoot. A blue gray heron nearly invisible in silvery gray branches. Night sounds settling in. It's good to be back. I feel like a monk as I walk behind you, tending a garden, sweeping fallen leaves, my eyes steadily down. Yesterday, at the Ginter Garden's Butterfly House, Abby was most interested in a young woman in brown, moving among the benches and feeders and flowering plants with a long broom, delicately gathering fallen blossoms and leaves, angling it over a butterfly on the floor when we walked a little too quickly in that direction. Overcast outside, drizzling. All around us the butterflies at rest, rising a few feet and then settling back, their wings seemingly steadying them from outside their own bodies. The broom, I think, gave her something to do with her hands as she drifted among us and answered questions. An artist I know has been sweeping a path across Will County, Illinois for the last four years, making his way, bit by bit, from Joliet to Crete. I've seen a video of him in 3-4 inches of new snow sweeping his way down an old railroad line set aside for bikers and walkers. He's moving towards us, almost at a steady walking pace, head down, sweeping across his body. There's an almost imperceptible pause at each step as he waits for the broom to fold in again across the center and then back out. He's focused on the rhythm and, through the rhythm, everything else. His breath mixes with the light. He moves towards us as if from another world, the hesitation in his stride the only sign that he's not quite at home here. The broom widens a seam cut by bikes in the snow just this side of dreaming. There's space now for two of us to move along it in the dark, eyes forward and down, attending.

Walking with my parents outside their house in Burlington. Signs everywhere of the driven, almost sideways rain that had torn through their neighborhood two days ago. Crepe myrtles stripped of their bark—flayed, curling lengths of it scattered across sidewalks and tiny patches of grass. We're heading up a hill toward the Memorial Garden where their ashes will be buried. They want to show us something there. Everything is so exposed—piles of bark heaped up and kicked apart by the wind, as if a desperate crowd at a border had suddenly been given a chance at life and had rushed through, abandoning everything. The exhilaration of it all. I had had an MRI yesterday for what turned out to be a torn meniscus and, watching my parents calmly drift away from me up the hill, I'm reminded of the feeling I'd had inside the scanner. I couldn't name it then. I had been given headphones and had asked for music to mute the potential claustrophobia, though I've always loved enclosed spaces. What surprised me was the feeling that washed over me when the violent whirring and banging began, taking the piano apart from within. It was as if a bolt had come loose in the lyric machinery itself, producing not chaos but some sort of wide brilliant opening, as if the music itself were holding its breath at its own undoing and peering across a border. I wanted to say something about that, but there was no need. They were already mostly up the hill, and there was no real occasion.

In the moment itself, I was simply and utterly lost. I suppose I had gotten turned around when I got up during the night, and when I turned back to where the bed should be, nothing. Two more steps and the nothing even deeper. Everything undone—you, me, the walls themselves—none of it real. It was only a moment, but it went on forever. Somehow I righted myself and slipped into bed. It's two hours later and I'm up again, in another room, blinking under a lamp. My heart still pounding. I need to get some of this down. It wasn't only terrifying. Something rose up there inside of me—not song exactly, though it moved that way, carried along on its own unfolding. "Use your words," my daughter says to her children when they get out ahead of themselves like this. In the myth, Psyche never sees the face of the god who comes to her at night. He is tender with her, rocking her, beautiful as the sea. He is Eros—Desire itself—though she doesn't know his name and has been told he's a monster. Who could leave it like that? Of course she looks, raising a lamp over the sleeping boy, hoping not to startle him, and is caught, banished, condemned to wander. And sees him everywhere, broken, partial, pieced out in words. Walking away. Turning back. The blind shifts, light on this page. "O my soul," she whispers. "Be in me now."

Down this hill, about a mile from where we've parked and picked up the trail, is a tree I love. It's dead, stripped of its bark, and a pale, washed silver. For years, it stood at an angle to the sky, tangled in another tree mid-fall, and on bright blue days its silver glowed blue when we approached it. I would wait for the moment after we picked our way across the bog at the bottom of the hill, turned slightly to the right and then caught sight of the tree. It wasn't always blue—time of day and conditions of the sky would determine that—and I think that's what I loved. That, and the casual way it had moved a strip of sky from one place to another. We're coming up on it now and I don't know if I'll say anything. It slipped completely to the ground a year ago and it doesn't matter, or matters in a different way. Its blue is gone. There's a hole cut out of the side of the trail where it would be, tugging at me a little. I remember how stuck I was, more than thirty-five years ago, working on my dissertation. I used to daydream about poking out an eye with a pencil so that I'd have a reason for just sitting on the couch and getting nowhere. This emptiness feels like that. What got me going again was playing around with a pair of scissors. I had a pile of photocopied chapters from Robert Duncan's unpublished *H.D. Book* that I'd found in little magazines in the library's Rare Book Room stacked up next to me, and I began cutting out paragraphs and then individual sentences, thinking I'd arrange them in various ways until they spoke to me and got me moving. Maybe they did. I've lost the paragraphs I'd saved, but I've hung on, all these years, to those yellowing pages with the holes cut out of them. Rectangles, little windows, Duncan's daybook entry March 13, Monday, 1961, for example, cut open once or twice on almost every page and speaking to me still. I think I was cutting shapes out of my emptiness. I couldn't tell you, back then, how much I was struggling and what I thought I saw there. But I can show you the pages—crinkled, black-bordered from the copier, the marks of the scissors sometimes bold, sometimes hesitatingly considering. Red underlines on the pages beneath still showing through, like the scarlet flowers near the inlet stream we know to look for this time of year.

NOTES

1. Wallace Stevens, "Of Modern Poetry"

2. Robert Duncan, "Often I Am Permitted to Return to a Meadow"

3. Robert Duncan, "A Poem Beginning with a Line by Pindar"

5. Wallace Stevens, "A Postcard from the Volcano"

6. Thomas Traherne, *Centuries of Meditations*

8. Elizabeth Bishop, "The Man-Moth"

10. Makoto Fujimura, "Water Flames Artist Talk"

12. Emily Dickinson, "In many and reportless places," "My period had come for Prayer—"; Robert Frost, "Out, Out—"

13. Ray Monk, *Ludwig Wittgenstein: The Duty of Genius*; Gertrude Stein, "A carafe, that is a blind glass"

14. Thomas Traherne, *Centuries of Meditations*; Job 38: 4, 7, as quoted in Malick's *The Tree of Life*

17. Virginia Woolf, *A Writer's Diary*

18. Walt Whitman, "Song of Myself," section 6

20. Thomas Traherne, *Centuries of Meditations*

23. Thomas Traherne, *Centuries of Meditations*; Wallace Stevens, "Peter Quince at the Clavier"

28. Psalm 42:5; Walt Whitman, "Song of Myself," section 5

33. Emily Dickinson, *Letters of Emily Dickinson*, number 871

37. Emily Dickinson, "It was not Death, for I stood up"

43. Walt Whitman, "A Glimpse"

44. William Carlos Williams, "The Botticellian Trees"

45. Emily Dickinson, "A Wife—at Daybreak—I shall be—"

46. Thomas Traherne, *Centuries of Meditations*

48. Emily Dickinson, "I stepped from Plank to Plank"

ACKNOWLEDGMENTS

My thanks to the following friends and colleagues who read these pieces along with me: Bob Braille, Fred Carlisle, Weston Cutter, Dan Gardner, Laura Gardner, Peter Graham, Bob Hicok, Cynthia Hogue, David Hopes, Tiffany Kriner, Glenn McLaughlin, Suzanne Nussey, Jamie Penven, Katy Powell, Karl Precoda, Patty Raun, Esther Richey, Bob Siegle, Edward Weisband, Matthew Vollmer.

Thanks as well to Peter Balakian and Bruce Smith who published selections from this book in *A Slant of Light: Reflections on Jack Wheatcroft* (Bucknell University Press, 2018).

Thomas Gardner has published five books of literary criticism and a previous collection of lyric essays from Tupelo entitled *Poverty Creek Journal*. He has been the recipient of Guggenheim, Fulbright, and National Endowment for the Arts fellowships. In 2003, he was awarded the Commonwealth of Virginia Outstanding Faculty Award. In 2006, his play *Eurydice* was performed at the Edinburgh Fringe Festival. He grew up in New Jersey and western Maryland, earned degrees from Bucknell, Syracuse, and the University of Wisconsin, and is Alumni Distinguished Professor of English at Virginia Tech, where he has taught for thirty-eight years. He and his wife live in Blacksburg, Virginia, on the edge of the Jefferson National Forest.

RECENT AND SELECTED TITLES FROM TUPELO PRESS

Poverty Creek Journal (lyric essay)
   by Thomas Gardner

Shahr-e-jaanaan: The City of The Beloved (poems)
   by Adeeba Shahid Talukder

The Nail in the Tree: Essays on Art, Violence, and Childhood (essays/visual studies)
   by Carol Ann Davis

Exclusions (poems)
   by Noah Falck

Arrows (poems)
   by Dan Beachy-Quick

Lucky Fish (poems)
   by Aimee Nezhukumatathil

Butterfly Sleep (drama)
   by Kim Kyung Ju, translated by Jake Levine

Canto General: Song of the Americas (poems)
   by Pablo Neruda, translated by Mariela Griffor with Jeffrey Levine,
   Nancy Naomi Carlson, and Rebecca Sieferle

Franciscan Notes (poems/memoir)
   by Alan Williamson

boysgirls (hybrid fiction)
   by Katie Farris

Diurne (poems)
   by Kristin George Bagdanov

America that island off the coast of France (poems)
   by Jesse Lee Kercheval

Epistle, Osprey (poems)
   by Geri Doran

Hazel (fiction)
   by David Huddle

See our complete list at tupelopress.org